MAKING MONEY WITH AI

THE BOOKYST

CHAPTER 1

INTRODUCTION AND HOW TO MAKE MONEY WITH AI

IN THE DIGITAL AGE, artificial intelligence (AI) is not just a buzzword but a pivotal technology reshaping every facet of our lives. From the way we communicate to how we work and entertain ourselves, AI's influence is omnipresent. This introductory chapter delves into the essence of AI and unfolds the myriad ways it can be leveraged to generate income online.

UNDERSTANDING AI

To harness AI effectively, it's essential to understand what it is and isn't. At its core, AI is a branch of computer science focused on creating systems that can learn, reason, and make decisions or predictions, mimicking human intelligence. It encompasses various technologies like machine learning, natural language processing, and robotics.

The common misconception that AI is a distant, futuristic concept needs to be dispelled. AI is here, and it's more accessible than ever. Tools and platforms incorporating AI are widely available, offering unprecedented opportunities to automate, optimize, and innovate in virtually every industry.

AI'S ECONOMIC IMPACT

The economic impact of AI is colossal. According to PwC, AI could contribute up to $15.7 trillion to the global economy by 2030. This staggering figure underscores the transformative potential of AI, not just for large corporations but for individuals and small businesses.

MAKING MONEY WITH AI

AI is not just a tool for efficiency and automation; it's a versatile ally in generating income online. Here's how you can capitalize on AI's capabilities in various domains:

Freelancing with AI: AI can augment your freelancing skills, especially in content creation and design. Whether it's generating written content, creating engaging graphics, or even developing entire websites, AI tools can enhance quality and speed, giving you a competitive edge.

AI in Stock Trading and Investment: AI's ability to analyze market trends and make predictions can be invaluable in stock trading and investment. By leveraging AI tools, you can gain insights into market movements, helping make more informed investment decisions.

Writing and Copywriting: AI's natural language processing capabilities are revolutionizing writing and copywriting. AI can assist in producing high-quality, engaging content, from blog posts to advertising copy, at a fraction of the time it would take manually.

Creating a Faceless YouTube Channel: AI can help you create a faceless YouTube channel, where content is generated through AI tools. This method is perfect for those who prefer to remain anonymous but want to produce engaging video content.

AI-Generated Blogs: For those interested in blogging, AI can automate the generation of blog posts on various topics. This can be particularly useful for maintaining a steady stream of content and attracting a consistent audience.

AI and Affiliate Marketing: AI can optimize affiliate marketing strategies. From identifying the right products to targeting the right audience, AI can enhance your affiliate marketing efforts, leading to increased income.

Building Websites with AI: AI tools can streamline the process of website development, from layout design to content creation. This opens up opportunities to offer website building services or create your own sites for various purposes.

Generating Art with AI: Artists and creatives can use AI to generate unique art pieces. This technology can create stunning visuals, which can then be sold as digital art, prints, or used in various other commercial applications.

Audio AI Income: Converting text content to audio using AI tools can open up new avenues like podcasts or audiobooks. This method is especially useful for repurposing existing content to reach a broader audience.

Each of these methods harnesses AI's power to create new or enhance existing revenue streams. As AI technology continues to evolve, so too will the opportunities to innovate and profit in the digital space.

SKILLS REQUIRED

To make money with AI, one doesn't necessarily need to be a tech wizard. A basic understanding of AI and how it applies to your field of interest is a good starting point. Continuous learning and adaptability are key, as the AI landscape is ever-evolving.

ETHICAL CONSIDERATIONS

While exploring AI's potential, it's crucial to consider the ethical implications. Issues like data privacy, bias in AI algorithms, and job displacement are vital to address. Ethical use of AI not only ensures compliance with regulations but also builds trust with your audience or customers.

AI'S ACCESSIBILITY

One of the most exciting aspects of AI today is its accessibility. Cloud- based AI services, open-source software, and user-friendly platforms have democratized access to AI technologies. This accessibility means that anyone with an internet connection and a willingness to learn can start leveraging AI to generate income.

THE FUTURE IS AI-DRIVEN

As we stand on the cusp of a new era, it's clear that AI will be a significant driver of economic growth and innovation. The businesses and individuals who adapt to this AI-driven world are the ones who will thrive.

CONCLUSION

AI offers a goldmine of opportunities for those willing to explore and innovate. This book aims to guide you through the labyrinth of possibilities AI presents, helping you unlock new avenues for income generation. As we delve deeper into specific applications of AI in the following chapters, remember that the journey of mastering AI for profit is as exciting as the destination.

CHAPTER 2

FREELANCING WITH AI: LEVERAGING AI TOOLS FOR CONTENT CREATION AND DESIGN

IN THE RAPIDLY EVOLVING WORLD OF freelancing, artificial intelligence (AI) has emerged as a game-changer, particularly in the realms of content creation and design. This chapter explores how freelancers can harness AI tools to elevate their work, streamline their processes, and stay ahead in a competitive market.

THE AI ADVANTAGE IN FREELANCING

The integration of AI into freelancing marks a significant shift from traditional methods. AI tools offer speed, efficiency, and a level of creativity that can augment a freelancer's capabilities. They can handle repetitive tasks, analyze large datasets for insights, and even aid in creative processes, allowing freelancers to focus on more complex aspects of their projects.

AI IN CONTENT CREATION

For freelance content creators, AI can be a powerful ally. AI-powered writing assistants can generate ideas, suggest improvements, and even write entire pieces based on given prompts. These tools use natural language processing (NLP) to understand and mimic human language, making the content they produce increasingly sophisticated and engaging.

Blog Writing: AI tools can generate blog posts on a variety of topics, helping maintain a steady content flow. This is particularly useful for managing multiple clients or keeping a personal blog updated.

Copywriting: In the world of advertising and marketing, AI can create compelling copy that resonates with target audiences. These tools can analyze consumer data to determine the most effective language and style.

SEO Optimization: AI can also assist in optimizing content for search engines, a crucial aspect for online visibility. By analyzing search trends and keywords, AI tools can guide content creators in crafting SEO-friendly material.

AI IN GRAPHIC DESIGN AND MULTIMEDIA

AI's impact extends beyond writing into the visual realm of graphic design and multimedia creation. AI tools in design can automate layout creation, suggest color palettes, and even generate entire designs based on brief descriptions.

Logo and Branding: AI can create unique logos and branding materials, offering a range of options based on a client's preferences and industry trends.

Web and UX/UI Design: AI tools can expedite the web design process, from wireframing to final design elements, ensuring a user- friendly experience.

Video Production: In video production, AI can assist in editing, adding effects, and even generating video content, which is especially useful for social media marketing.

THE HUMAN-AI COLLABORATION

A key aspect of leveraging AI in freelancing is understanding the collaborative relationship between human creativity and AI efficiency. While AI can handle certain tasks, the human touch is essential for originality, emotional intelligence, and nuanced understanding of client needs. Successful freelancers will find a balance, using AI to enhance their skills rather than replace them.

LEARNING AND ADAPTING TO AI TOOLS

To effectively incorporate AI into freelancing, one must be willing to learn and adapt. Many AI tools are user-friendly, but they do require a basic understanding of their capabilities and limitations. Online courses, tutorials, and community forums can be invaluable resources for keeping up with the latest AI advancements

BUILDING A PORTFOLIO WITH AI

Freelancers can use AI to build and diversify their portfolios. By showcasing work that integrates AI, freelancers can demonstrate
their proficiency in modern techniques, attracting clients looking for cutting-edge skills.

ETHICAL CONSIDERATIONS AND TRANSPARENCY

When using AI, freelancers must consider ethical implications and be transparent with clients about AI usage. This includes issues related to data privacy, intellectual property, and the authenticity of the work. Clear communication about the role of AI in the creative process is essential for maintaining trust and integrity in the freelance community.

STAYING AHEAD OF THE CURVE

The field of AI is constantly evolving, and freelancers need to stay informed about new tools and technologies. Networking with other professionals, participating in online forums, and attending industry events can help freelancers stay ahead of the curve.

THE FUTURE OF FREELANCING WITH AI

As AI technology advances, its role in freelancing will continue to grow. Freelancers who embrace AI tools will find themselves better equipped to handle diverse projects, scale their businesses, and offer innovative solutions to their clients.

AI is not just a technological advancement; it's a paradigm shift in the freelance world. By leveraging AI tools for content creation and design, freelancers can enhance their creativity, increase their productivity, and open new avenues for growth and success. This chapter serves as a guide for freelancers to navigate the AI landscape, helping them harness its power to transform their freelance careers.

CHAPTER 3

AI IN STOCK TRADING AND INVESTMENT: ANALYZING TRENDS AND MAKING PREDICTIONS

IN THE INTRICATE world of stock trading and investment, Artificial Intelligence (AI) is revolutionizing how market analysis is performed and decisions are made. This chapter delves into the application of AI in stock trading and investment, focusing on how it aids in analyzing trends and making predictions.

THE ROLE OF AI IN MODERN INVESTMENT STRATEGIES

The integration of AI into the financial sector has brought about a paradigm shift in how investments are managed. AI's ability to process vast amounts of data quickly and accurately enables investors to make more informed decisions. Machine learning algorithms, a subset of AI, are particularly adept at identifying patterns and trends in the market, often unnoticed by human analysts.

UNDERSTANDING MACHINE LEARNING IN TRADING

Machine learning in trading involves the use of algorithms that can learn from and make predictions based on data. These algorithms are fed historical market data, and they use this information to predict future market trends. The predictive power of AI becomes a valuable asset in making strategic trading decisions.

Algorithmic Trading: AI drives algorithmic trading, where decisions to buy or sell stocks are made automatically, based on pre-set criteria. These algorithms can analyze market data at a speed and accuracy that is impossible for human traders.

Risk Management: AI algorithms can also be programmed to understand and manage risks. They can adjust trading strategies based on market volatility and other risk factors, helping to minimize losses.

Portfolio Management: AI systems can manage entire investment portfolios, known as robo-advisors. They allocate assets based on the investor's risk tolerance and investment goals, continuously optimizing the portfolio for maximum return.

PREDICTIVE ANALYTICS IN STOCK TRADING

Predictive analytics involves using statistical techniques and algorithms to analyze current and historical data to make predictions about future events. In stock trading, this means predicting market movements, stock prices, or economic trends.

Market Trend Analysis: AI can analyze news articles, financial reports, and social media to gauge market sentiment. This analysis can predict how certain events will impact the stock market.

Price Prediction: AI models are used to predict future stock prices based on historical price data and other relevant economic indicators.

THE ADVANTAGES OF AI OVER TRADITIONAL METHODS

Traditional methods of stock analysis, such as fundamental and technical analysis, are limited by the amount of data a human can process. AI, on the other hand, can analyze enormous datasets, spot trends, and even learn from its analysis, improving its accuracy over time.

Speed and Efficiency: AI can process and analyze data much faster than any human trader, providing real-time insights.

Eliminating Human Bias: AI relies purely on

data and algorithms, eliminating emotional and cognitive biases that often affect human traders.

Backtesting: AI allows investors to backtest trading strategies using historical data, providing a safe way to evaluate the effectiveness of a strategy without risking actual capital.

CHALLENGES AND LIMITATIONS OF AI IN TRADING

While AI offers many advantages, it's important to be aware of its limitations. AI systems are only as good as the data they are trained on. Poor quality or biased data can lead to inaccurate predictions. Moreover, AI algorithms can be complex, and their decision-making processes are not always transparent, making it difficult to understand why certain decisions are made.

ETHICAL AND REGULATORY CONSIDERATIONS

The rise of AI in trading also brings ethical and regulatory challenges. Issues such as data privacy, market manipulation, and the potential for AI-driven market instability need to be addressed. Regulators are increasingly focusing on AI in financial markets to ensure fair and transparent trading practices.

PREPARING FOR AN AI-DRIVEN FUTURE IN TRADING

For those looking to leverage AI in their trading strategies, it's important to stay informed about the latest developments in AI and finance. This involves continuous learning and adapting to new tools and methodologies. Collaborating with AI experts and participating in financial technology communities can also provide valuable insights.

AI is transforming the landscape of stock trading and investment, offering tools and techniques that were unimaginable a few decades ago. By harnessing the power of AI for analyzing trends and making predictions, investors and traders can achieve a level of precision and efficiency that enhances their decision-making process. As the technology continues to evolve, so too will the strategies and successes of those who embrace it.

CHAPTER 4

CREATING A FACELESS YOUTUBE CHANNEL WITH AI

IN THE EVOLVING landscape of online content creation, the concept of a 'faceless' YouTube channel, where creators remain anonymous while producing engaging content, is gaining popularity. Artificial Intelligence (AI) plays a pivotal role in this domain, offering innovative ways to create and manage such channels. This chapter explores the ins and outs of utilizing AI to create a successful faceless YouTube channel.

UNDERSTANDING FACELESS YOUTUBE CHANNELS

A faceless YouTube channel is one where the identity of the content creator remains hidden. These channels typically rely on narrations, animations, and AI-generated content. The appeal lies in the creator's ability to maintain privacy while still engaging a wide audience.

WHY CHOOSE A FACELESS CHANNEL?

The reasons for choosing a faceless approach vary. For some, it's a matter of privacy and security; for others, it's about focusing solely on the content rather than the creator. Additionally, it allows creators to produce a diverse range of content without being limited by personal expertise or appearance.

LEVERAGING AI IN CONTENT CREATION

Scriptwriting and Narration: AI-powered tools can assist in scriptwriting by generating ideas or even entire scripts based on specific keywords or themes. Text-to-speech technology can then be used to narrate these scripts, offering a variety of voices and languages.

Animation and Video Production: AI can create animations or compile video footage based on the script. This technology ranges from simple slide-based videos to more complex animated explainers.

Editing and Post-Production: AI tools can also aid in editing by suggesting cuts, transitions, and even integrating background music that fits the video's mood and tone.

CONTENT IDEATION WITH AI

Utilizing AI for content ideation involves leveraging AI tools to generate topic ideas, titles, and even keywords for SEO optimization. This can be particularly useful in keeping the content fresh and aligned with current trends and search patterns.

Trend Analysis: AI can analyze current trends on YouTube and social media to suggest relevant and popular topics.

Keyword Optimization: AI tools can suggest keywords to include in the video title, description, and tags, which is crucial for SEO and ensuring the content reaches the target audience.

BUILDING AND MANAGING THE CHANNEL

Creating the content is just one part of running a YouTube channel. AI can assist in channel management tasks such as:

Audience Analysis: AI can analyze viewer data to understand audience preferences, helping to tailor future content to viewer interests.

Comment Moderation: AI can help manage and moderate comments, ensuring a positive and constructive community.

Scheduling and Publishing: AI tools can suggest the best times to publish videos based on when the target audience is most active.

MONETIZATION STRATEGIES

For a faceless YouTube channel, monetization can come from various sources:

Ad Revenue: The primary source of income for many YouTubers comes from ads displayed on their videos.

Sponsored Content: AI can help identify potential sponsorship opportunities by analyzing which brands or products are a good fit for the channel's audience.

Affiliate Marketing: AI tools can suggest products or services for affiliate marketing based on the content of the videos and the interests of the audience.

CHALLENGES AND CONSIDERATIONS

Running a faceless YouTube channel with AI comes with its set of challenges:

Content Quality: Ensuring the AI-generated content maintains high quality and originality is crucial. Over-reliance on AI can lead to repetitive or uninspired content.

Ethical Considerations: The use of AI in content creation raises questions about authenticity and transparency. Creators should be clear about their use of AI and ensure compliance with YouTube's policies.

Keeping Up with AI Advancements: The field of AI is rapidly evolving. Creators need to stay informed about the latest developments in AI tools and technologies.

Creating a faceless YouTube channel with the aid of AI is a journey that combines creativity, technology, and strategic thinking. This approach offers a unique opportunity to produce diverse and engaging content while maintaining the creator's privacy. By leveraging AI for tasks ranging from content creation to channel management and monetization, creators can efficiently manage their channels and potentially reach a vast audience. As AI technology continues to evolve, so too will the opportunities for innovative content creation on platforms like YouTube.

CHAPTER 5

USING AI TO PROVIDE WRITING AND COPYWRITING

IN THE DYNAMIC world of digital content, the use of Artificial Intelligence (AI) in writing and copywriting is transforming the landscape. This chapter delves into how AI is being employed to revolutionize the way written content is produced, from blogs and articles to advertising copy and social media content.

THE RISE OF AI IN WRITING

The emergence of AI in the field of writing marks a significant shift from traditional content creation methods. AI writing tools, powered by advanced algorithms and natural language processing (NLP) capabilities, are capable of producing coherent, engaging, and contextually relevant text. This technology is not only enhancing the efficiency of content creation but also opening new avenues for creativity and experimentation.

UNDERSTANDING AI WRITING TOOLS

AI writing tools are software programs that can generate text based on input parameters. These tools use machine learning algorithms to understand language patterns and structures, enabling them to create content that closely resembles human writing. Some popular AI writing tools include GPT-3 (Generative Pre-trained Transformer 3), BERT (Bidirectional Encoder Representations from Transformers), and others.

APPLICATIONS OF AI IN WRITING AND COPYWRITING

Content Generation: AI can generate articles, blog posts, and even books, based on specified topics and styles. This can be particularly useful for maintaining a consistent flow of content on websites and blogs.

Copywriting: In the world of marketing, AI tools can produce compelling ad copy, product descriptions, and promotional content tailored to specific audiences and objectives.

SEO Optimization: AI can assist in crafting content that is optimized for search engines, incorporating relevant keywords, and maintaining an appropriate keyword density without compromising the natural flow of the text.

Personalized Content: AI can be used to create personalized content for different segments of an audience, enhancing the effectiveness of marketing campaigns and customer engagement.

BENEFITS OF USING AI FOR WRITING

The integration of AI into writing brings several benefits:

Efficiency and Productivity: AI tools can generate content quickly, enabling writers and marketers to produce more content in less time.

Consistency: AI ensures a consistent tone and style across various pieces of content, which is crucial for brand identity and messaging.

Scalability: AI allows for the scalability of content production, which is particularly beneficial for businesses and organizations with large content needs.

Cost-Effectiveness: AI-driven content creation can be more cost- effective than hiring multiple writers, especially for large-scale projects.

ENHANCING CREATIVITY, NOT REPLACING IT

While AI can significantly aid in the writing process, it is important to note that it complements human creativity rather than replacing it. The most effective use of AI in writing involves a collaborative approach, where human oversight and creative input guide the AI- generated content to ensure originality, relevance, and emotional appeal.

CHALLENGES AND CONSIDERATIONS

Using AI for writing also comes with its challenges:

Quality Control: While AI can produce content quickly, the quality of the output may vary. Human editing and review are essential to ensure the content meets the desired standards.

Ethical Concerns: The use of AI in writing raises ethical questions about authorship and originality. Transparency about the use of AI in content creation is important.

Overreliance on AI: Relying too heavily on AI for content creation can lead to a lack of uniqueness and personal touch in the writing, which can be crucial in certain contexts.

STAYING AHEAD IN THE AI WRITING SPACE

To effectively use AI in writing and copywriting, it is important to stay informed about the latest developments and best practices. Continuous learning, experimenting with different AI tools, and integrating AI strategically into the content creation process are key to leveraging AI effectively.

AI is rapidly transforming the field of writing and copywriting, offering new possibilities for content creation that are efficient, scalable, and innovative. By understanding and embracing the capabilities of AI writing tools, writers, marketers, and businesses can enhance their content production and engage their audiences in more meaningful ways. As AI technology continues to evolve, so too will the opportunities and approaches to AI-driven writing and copywriting.

CHAPTER 6

MAKING MONEY WITH AI-GENERATED BLOGS

THE ADVENT of AI-generated content has opened new avenues for bloggers and content creators. In this chapter, we explore how AI can be utilized to create compelling blog content and the various strategies to monetize these AI-generated blogs effectively.

THE INTERSECTION OF AI AND BLOGGING

Blogging, traditionally a platform for individuals to express ideas and share knowledge, has evolved into a lucrative business model. The integration of AI into blogging accelerates content creation, offering unique opportunities for monetization. AI-generated blogs can cover a wide range of topics, from niche subjects to more popular themes, with the added advantage of producing content at a significantly faster rate than manual writing.

UNDERSTANDING AI-GENERATED CONTENT

AI-generated content is created using algorithms and machine learning models that can write articles, stories, and even technical content. These AI models are trained on large datasets, enabling them to generate coherent and contextually relevant content. While not without limitations, AI-generated content can be an efficient way to produce high volumes of blog posts.

SETTING UP AN AI-GENERATED BLOG

Choosing a Niche: Selecting a specific niche is crucial. AI can generate content on various topics, but a focused niche often attracts a more dedicated audience.

AI Content Generation Tools: Tools like OpenAI's GPT-3 are popular for creating blog content. These tools can be fine-tuned to match the style and tone appropriate for the chosen niche.

Integrating AI with CMS: Many content management systems (CMS) can integrate with AI writing tools, streamlining the content creation process.

Wordpress may be one of the best CMS due the flexibility, ideal for creating content with AI Plugins.

MONETIZING AI-GENERATED BLOGS

Advertising: Display ads are a common monetization strategy. With high-quality, AI-generated content attracting traffic, ad revenue can increase significantly.

Affiliate Marketing: AI-generated blogs can effectively promote products or services. By integrating affiliate links within the content, bloggers can earn commissions on sales.

Sponsored Content: Companies often pay for sponsored posts on popular blogs. AI-generated blogs with substantial traffic can attract such sponsorship opportunities.

Subscription Models: Offering premium content through subscriptions can be a lucrative model. AI can help in creating this exclusive content, tailored to subscriber interests.

QUALITY AND AUTHENTICITY IN AI-GENERATED CONTENT

While AI can produce content efficiently, ensuring quality and authenticity is vital.

Editing and Reviewing: AI-generated content

should be reviewed and edited by human editors to ensure it meets quality standards and resonates with the audience.

Avoiding Plagiarism: It's crucial to ensure the AI-generated content is original and not plagiarized. Using plagiarism checkers can help maintain the integrity of the blog.

Balancing AI and Human Touch: The best AI-generated blogs strike a balance between AI efficiency and human creativity. Personal insights, experiences, or interpretations added to AI-generated content can enhance its value.

SEO OPTIMIZATION FOR AI BLOGS

To ensure the blog reaches its intended audience, SEO optimization is key.

Keyword Research: Using AI tools for keyword research can help identify the terms and phrases your target audience is searching for.

SEO-friendly Content: AI tools can optimize content for SEO, but human oversight is needed to ensure that the content remains engaging and readable.

CHALLENGES AND ETHICAL CONSIDERATIONS

Using AI in blogging presents challenges and ethical considerations.

Dependence on AI: Over-reliance on AI for content generation can lead to a lack of diversity in writing styles and perspectives.

Transparency: It's important to be transparent about the use of AI in content creation, particularly if the blog positions itself as an expert or authoritative source.

Navigating Algorithm Updates: Search engine algorithms continually evolve, and AI-generated content must adapt to these changes to maintain visibility and relevance.

STAYING AHEAD IN AI BLOGGING

Staying informed about the latest developments in AI and content creation is crucial.

Continuous Learning: Regularly updating skills and knowledge about AI tools and content strategies is essential.

Community Engagement: Participating in blogging and AI communities can provide insights and help keep up with trends and best practices.

AI-generated blogs offer a promising avenue for content creators to produce diverse and frequent content, opening up numerous monetization opportunities. While AI facilitates efficiency in content creation, the human element in editing, ethical considerations, and creative input remains indispensable. As AI technology advances, so too will the strategies for creating and monetizing AI-generated blog content.

CHAPTER 7

BOOST YOUR INCOME WITH AI AND AFFILIATE MARKETING

AFFILIATE MARKETING, a strategy where businesses pay external websites to generate traffic or sales, has been revolutionized by Artificial Intelligence (AI). This chapter explores how AI can be leveraged in affiliate marketing to enhance strategies, optimize campaigns, and ultimately boost income.

UNDERSTANDING AFFILIATE MARKETING IN THE AI ERA

Affiliate marketing involves promoting products or services and earning a commission for every sale or lead generated. AI transforms this process by providing deep insights into consumer behavior, automating tasks, and personalizing marketing strategies, thus increasing the effectiveness and profitability of affiliate campaigns.

LEVERAGING AI FOR ENHANCED AFFILIATE MARKETING

Data Analysis and Consumer Insights: AI excels in analyzing large datasets. In affiliate marketing, AI can process consumer data to identify buying patterns, preferences, and trends. These insights allow for more targeted and effective marketing strategies.

Personalized Content Creation: AI tools can generate personalized content for different segments of your target audience, making your affiliate marketing efforts more relevant and engaging.

SEO Optimization: AI can optimize your content for search engines, increasing the visibility of your affiliate products or services. By analyzing search trends and keywords, AI tools can help create content that ranks higher in search results.

Automated Email Marketing: AI can automate and personalize email marketing campaigns based on user behavior and preferences, increasing open rates and click-through rates for affiliate links.

Chatbots for Enhanced Customer Engagement: AI-powered chatbots can interact with visitors on your website, providing product recommendations and answering queries, which can lead to increased affiliate sales.

STRATEGIES FOR MAXIMIZING INCOME WITH AI IN AFFILIATE MARKETING

Choosing the Right Affiliate Products: Use AI to analyze market trends and consumer demands to select affiliate products that are likely to resonate with your audience.

Optimizing Affiliate Websites: AI tools can analyze user behavior on your website, suggesting layout changes, content updates, and call- to-action placements to maximize conversions.

A/B Testing: AI can automate the process of A/B testing different aspects of your affiliate marketing campaigns, from email subject lines to landing page designs, ensuring that you always use the most effective strategies.

Tracking and Analytics: AI systems can track the performance of your affiliate campaigns in real-time, providing insights that can be used to optimize strategies and improve ROI.

THE HUMAN-AI SYNERGY IN AFFILIATE MARKETING

While AI provides powerful tools for data analysis and automation, the human touch is still crucial in affiliate marketing. Human intuition, creativity, and emotional intelligence are necessary to design compelling campaigns, create engaging content, and build relationships with customers.

CHALLENGES AND ETHICAL CONSIDERATIONS

Dependency on Technology: Over-reliance on AI can make affiliate marketers less attuned to nuanced changes in consumer behavior that AI might not yet recognize.

Data Privacy and Ethical Use: Ensuring that data is used ethically and in compliance with privacy laws is crucial. Transparent practices are essential to maintain consumer trust.

Keeping Up with AI Developments: The field of AI is rapidly evolving. Staying updated with the latest tools and techniques is essential for maximizing the benefits of AI in affiliate marketing.

BUILDING A SUCCESSFUL AI-DRIVEN AFFILIATE MARKETING BUSINESS

Continuous Learning and Adaptation: To stay competitive, affiliate marketers must continuously learn about new AI technologies and adapt their strategies accordingly.

Networking and Community Engagement: Engaging with other affiliate marketers and AI professionals can provide valuable insights and help you stay ahead of trends.

Experimentation: Be open to experimenting with different AI tools and strategies to find what works best for your specific niche and audience.

AI has the potential to significantly boost the effectiveness and profitability of affiliate marketing campaigns. By harnessing AI's power for data analysis, content creation, and campaign optimization, affiliate marketers can achieve greater efficiency and higher conversion rates. However, balancing AI capabilities with human creativity and ethical considerations is key to building a successful and sustainable affiliate marketing business.

CHAPTER 8

BUILDING WEBSITES WITH AI FOR INCOME

IN THE DIGITAL AGE, websites are essential for businesses, entrepreneurs, and creatives. The advent of Artificial Intelligence (AI) has revolutionized website building, making it more accessible, efficient, and profitable. This chapter explores how AI can be utilized to build websites and generate income, transforming traditional web development processes.

THE EVOLUTION OF WEB DEVELOPMENT WITH AI

Web development has traditionally required extensive coding knowledge and design expertise. However, AI has democratized this process by enabling the creation of sophisticated websites without the need for deep technical skills. AI-powered website builders can automate design, optimize user experience, and even handle SEO, allowing more individuals to enter the web development space and monetize their skills.

LEVERAGING AI IN WEBSITE BUILDING

AI-Powered Design Tools: AI can analyze design trends and user preferences to suggest website layouts, color schemes, and fonts, streamlining the design process.

Content Generation: AI tools can create written content for websites, from product descriptions to blog posts, tailored to the site's audience and SEO needs.

User Experience Optimization: AI can track user interactions and provide insights on how to improve the website for a better user experience, leading to higher engagement and conversion rates.

Automated SEO: AI can optimize websites for search engines, suggesting keywords, and analyzing competitor strategies, which is vital for online visibility.

MONETIZING AI-BUILT WEBSITES

Selling AI-Built Websites: There is a market for ready-made websites. Designing and selling AI-built websites can be a lucrative business, especially for niche markets.

Affiliate Marketing Websites: Using AI to build affiliate marketing websites can increase efficiency and profitability. AI can assist in identifying profitable niches and optimizing content for target audiences.

E-commerce Platforms: Building AI-powered e-commerce sites can enhance customer experience through personalized recommendations and optimized search functionality, driving sales.

Subscription-Based Models: Creating websites with exclusive, AI- generated content accessible via subscription can be a steady source of income.

THE HUMAN-AI COLLABORATION IN WEB DEVELOPMENT

While AI significantly streamlines web development, the human touch remains crucial. A successful AI-built website requires human oversight to ensure that it meets specific client needs, maintains a unique brand identity, and provides a genuinely engaging user experience.

CHALLENGES AND CONSIDERATIONS

Quality Control: Ensuring the quality of AI-generated content and designs is essential. Human expertise is needed to review and refine AI outputs.

Customization Limits: While AI can provide a

solid foundation for website design, it may have limitations in customization. Understanding these limitations is crucial for developers to intervene where necessary.

Staying Informed: The field of AI in web development is rapidly evolving. Keeping abreast of the latest tools and trends is vital to stay competitive.

NAVIGATING THE ETHICAL LANDSCAPE

Data Privacy: When using AI tools that collect user data, it's important to adhere to privacy laws and ethical standards.

Transparency: Being transparent about the use of AI in website building, especially if the AI influences content creation or user interaction, is crucial to maintain trust.

BUILDING A BUSINESS AROUND AI WEBSITE DEVELOPMENT

Target Market Identification: Understanding your target market and their specific needs can help tailor your AI web development services effectively.

Marketing Your Services: Utilize digital marketing strategies to promote your AI website building services. Showcasing a portfolio of AI-built websites can attract potential clients.

Continuous Learning and Skill Development:

The landscape of AI and web development is constantly changing. Continuous learning is crucial to adapt to new technologies and maintain a competitive edge.

AI's integration into website building opens up new opportunities for income generation in the digital space. By leveraging AI for design, content creation, and optimization, individuals can create high-quality websites with less effort and in a shorter timeframe. However, success in this field requires balancing AI efficiency with human creativity and ethical considerations. As AI technology continues to evolve, so does the potential for innovative and profitable web development.

CHAPTER 9

USING AI ART TO GENERATE MONEY ONLINE

THE INTERSECTION of Artificial Intelligence (AI) and art is creating groundbreaking opportunities for artists and entrepreneurs. AI art, where algorithms create or assist in creating visual art, has opened a new frontier in the digital art market. This chapter explores how AI art can be created and monetized in today's online landscape.

UNDERSTANDING AI ART

AI art involves using algorithms to create artwork that can range from digital paintings and illustrations to complex 3D models and even interactive visual experiences. These algorithms, often based on neural networks, can analyze thousands of existing artworks to learn specific styles and then apply these styles to create new, unique pieces.

CREATING AI ART

Generative Adversarial Networks (GANs): GANs are a popular method for creating AI art. They involve two neural networks — one generating art and the other evaluating it — working in tandem to produce visually appealing results.

Deep Learning and Style Transfer: AI can analyze artistic styles from various eras and artists and apply them to new creations, leading to innovative pieces that blend traditional styles with contemporary concepts.

Collaborative AI Art: Artists can collaborate with AI, using it as a tool to expand their creativity. The AI can suggest modifications, compositions, or even color schemes, enhancing the artist's original vision.

MONETIZING AI ART

Selling AI Art Online: Digital platforms like Etsy, Saatchi Art, and even dedicated NFT (Non-Fungible Token) marketplaces offer venues to sell AI-generated artwork.

Print-on-Demand Services: AI art can be sold as physical prints through print-on-demand services. This method allows artists to sell worldwide without worrying about inventory or shipping.

Licensing AI Art: AI-generated images can be

licensed for use in advertising, media, or as part of digital products, providing a recurring income stream.

Custom AI Art Services: Offering custom AI art creation services can attract clients looking for unique artwork for personal or professional use.

BUILDING A BRAND AROUND AI ART

Online Presence: Creating a strong online presence through a dedicated website and social media platforms is crucial. Platforms like Instagram and Pinterest are particularly effective for visual art.

Storytelling: Sharing the story behind the AI art, the process, and the technology can engage audiences and create more value for the artwork.

Networking in the Art Community: Engaging with both traditional and digital art communities can open up opportunities for collaborations, exhibitions, and sales.

CHALLENGES IN AI ART

Public Perception and Acceptance: AI art challenges traditional notions of creativity and authorship, which can affect its acceptance in the art community.

Quality and Uniqueness: While AI can generate art, ensuring that each piece is unique and of high quality can be challenging. Artists need to curate and refine AI-generated art carefully.

Ethical Considerations: The use of AI in art raises questions about originality and the future of human creativity in the arts. It's important to navigate these ethical considerations thoughtfully.

STAYING AHEAD IN THE AI ART MARKET

Continuous Learning: The field of AI art is rapidly evolving. Staying informed about the latest technologies and artistic trends is essential.

Experimentation: Experimenting with different AI tools and techniques can lead to unique and innovative artwork.

Collaboration: Collaborating with other AI artists, technologists, and traditional artists can lead to new insights and opportunities.

AI art represents a novel and exciting frontier in the digital art world. By leveraging AI to create and enhance artwork, artists and entrepreneurs can tap into new markets and audiences. However, success in this field requires not just an understanding of the technology but also an approach that respects and enhances the artistic process. As AI continues to evolve, so too will the opportunities and challenges in creating and monetizing AI art.

CHAPTER 10

AUDIO AI INCOME - CONVERTING CONTENT TO AUDIO WITH AI TOOLS

THE RISE of audio content in the digital era has been meteoric, with podcasts, audiobooks, and AI-generated voiceovers becoming increasingly popular. This chapter delves into how Artificial Intelligence (AI) can be leveraged to convert written content into audio, creating new revenue streams for content creators.

THE GROWING DEMAND FOR AUDIO CONTENT

In today's fast-paced world, more people are turning to audio content for its convenience and accessibility. From educational material to entertainment, audio content allows users to multitask and consume information on the go. This shift has created a lucrative market for audio versions of written content.

UNDERSTANDING AI IN AUDIO CONVERSION

AI in audio conversion involves using text-to-speech (TTS) technologies. These AI tools can read written text aloud, mimicking human voices with increasing accuracy. Modern TTS systems offer a range of voices, accents, and languages, making audio content more personal and engaging.

CREATING AI-GENERATED AUDIO CONTENT

Converting Blogs and Articles: Transforming written blogs or articles into podcasts or audio articles can attract a wider audience and cater to those who prefer listening over reading.

Audiobooks and Narratives: AI can convert novels, short stories, and other literary works into audiobooks, opening up a new channel for authors and publishers.

Educational Material: AI-generated audio can be used to create educational and training materials, making learning more accessible for various audiences.

MONETIZING AI-GENERATED AUDIO CONTENT

Podcast Platforms: Platforms like Spotify, Apple Podcasts, and Google Podcasts are popular for hosting and monetizing podcasts. AI-generated audio content can be distributed through these platforms.

Subscription Services: Offering exclusive AI-generated audio content through subscription models can provide a steady income stream.

Advertising and Sponsorships: Incorporating ads or sponsor messages into AI-generated audio content can generate additional revenue.

Selling Audiobooks: Platforms like Audible and Google Play Books provide avenues to sell AI-generated audiobooks.

QUALITY AND AUTHENTICITY IN AI AUDIO

Ensuring high-quality and authentic AI-generated audio is crucial:

Selecting the Right AI Tool: Choosing an AI TTS tool that offers natural-sounding voices and customization options is essential for creating engaging audio content.

Editing and Enhancing Audio: Post-production editing is vital to refine the AI-generated audio, removing any errors and adding music or sound effects if needed.

Balancing AI and Human Touch: While AI can generate the bulk of the audio content, adding human-recorded introductions or conclusions can personalize the content and enhance listener engagement.

CHALLENGES IN AI-GENERATED AUDIO

Ethical Considerations: Transparency about the use of AI in generating audio content is important. Listeners should be aware if the content they are consuming is AI-generated.

Keeping Up with Technology: AI in audio is a rapidly evolving field. Staying updated with the latest advancements is crucial to maintain the quality and relevance of the audio content.

Market Saturation: With the increasing popularity of audio content, standing out in a crowded market can be challenging. Creating unique and high-quality content is key.

MARKETING AI-GENERATED AUDIO CONTENT

Social Media Promotion: Utilizing social media platforms to promote AI-generated audio content can reach a broad audience.

Collaborations and Partnerships: Collaborating with influencers, other content creators, or brands can increase the visibility of the audio content.

SEO for Audio Content: Optimizing the content for search engines, including relevant keywords in the descriptions and tags, can improve discoverability.

BUILDING A BUSINESS AROUND AI-GENERATED AUDIO

Understanding the Audience: Knowing the target audience and their preferences is essential for creating content that resonates and attracts listeners.

Diversifying Content: Offering a variety of content, from educational to entertainment, can attract a wider audience base.

Continuous Learning: Keeping abreast of trends in the audio content market and technological advancements in AI is crucial for success.

The integration of AI in converting written content to audio presents exciting opportunities for content creators to diversify their offerings and tap into new income streams. By leveraging AI tools, creators can efficiently produce high-quality audio content that meets the growing demand for auditory experiences. While embracing these new technologies, maintaining a balance between automation and the human element is key to creating content that is both engaging and authentic.

CHAPTER 11

USING CHAT GPT PROMPTS TO IMPROVE YOUR PROJECT

A CHATGPT PROMPT is a statement or a set of instructions provided to the ChatGPT model to generate a response. It serves as the input to the language model, guiding it to produce text that is relevant to the given prompt. The prompt essentially frames the conversation or the task at hand, helping the model understand the context and generate coherent and relevant responses. Users can craft prompts to initiate dialogue, ask questions, or request specific types of content from the model.

HOW TO USE PROMPTS FOR BUSINESS ACTIVITIES?

Writing prompts for business activities involves providing clear instructions or questions that guide the conversation towards topics relevant to business operations, strategies, decision-making, or any other related aspects. Here are some tips for writing prompts for business activities:

- **Be Clear and Specific**: Clearly outline the purpose of the conversation or the specific topic you want to address. Ambiguity can lead to irrelevant responses.
- **Provide Context**: Give background information or context relevant to the business activity you want to discuss. This helps the model understand the scope of the conversation.
- **Ask Direct Questions**: Pose questions that require specific answers related to the business activity. For example: "What are the key factors to consider when developing a marketing strategy?" "How can businesses improve customer retention rates?" "What are the latest trends in supply chain management?"
- **Use Scenarios**: Present hypothetical scenarios or situations that reflect real-world business challenges. This can help generate responses that offer practical insights or solutions. For example: "Imagine a startup looking to raise

funding. What are some effective strategies for approaching investors?" "A company is experiencing a decline in sales. How can they identify the root causes and implement corrective measures?"

- **Encourage Analysis and Evaluation**: Prompt the model to analyze data, evaluate options, or provide recommendations based on business principles or best practices. For example: "Compare and contrast the advantages and disadvantages of different pricing strategies." "Evaluate the potential risks and benefits of expanding into new markets."

- **Include Constraints or Parameters**: If applicable, specify any constraints or parameters relevant to the discussion. This helps focus the conversation on practical and feasible solutions. For example: "Considering a limited budget, propose cost-effective marketing tactics for a small business." "Discuss strategies for improving workplace productivity while maintaining work-life balance."

- **Allow for Open-Ended Exploration**: While specificity is

important, also leave room for open-ended exploration and creativity. This can lead to unexpected insights or innovative ideas. For example: "Explore emerging technologies that could disrupt traditional business models." "Discuss the future of remote work and its implications for organizational structure and culture."
- **Iterate and Refine**: Continuously refine your prompts based on the responses you receive. Pay attention to the relevance and quality of the generated content, and adjust your prompts accordingly to elicit more informative or insightful responses.

By following these guidelines, you can effectively craft prompts that stimulate meaningful discussions and generate valuable insights for business activities.

SIMPLE STRUCTURE OF A GOOD PROMPT

A good prompt for business activities should be structured in a clear and concise manner to effectively guide the conversation and elicit relevant responses. Here's a suggested structure for crafting such prompts:

- **Introduction/Context**: Start by providing a brief introduction or context to set the stage for the conversation. This helps the model understand the purpose and scope of the prompt. Example: "In the context of marketing strategies for small businesses..."
- **Specific Question or Instruction**: Clearly state the main question or instruction that you want the model to address. Be precise and direct to ensure clarity. Example: "What are the most effective digital marketing tactics for small businesses with limited budgets?"
- **Clarifying Details (if necessary)**: If the prompt requires specific details or constraints, provide them here to guide the response. Example: "Considering a budget of $5,000 per month, discuss actionable strategies that prioritize ROI."
- **Optional: Additional Context or Examples**: Offer additional context, examples, or scenarios to further illustrate the topic and stimulate discussion. Example: "For instance, how could a local bakery leverage social media platforms to increase brand visibility and attract more customers?"
- **Closing/Encouragement for**

Insightful Responses: Conclude the prompt by encouraging thoughtful and insightful responses. Example: "We're looking for practical recommendations backed by industry insights and best practices."

By following this structured approach, you can create prompts that effectively guide the conversation and prompt the model to generate informative and relevant responses tailored to the specific business activity or topic at hand.

CHAPTER 12

CHAT GPT PROMPTS EXAMPLE

WRITING prompts from scratch could be challenging, that's why I am going to share with you some prompts you can use to make provide marketing and business consultancy or to use them in your own project.

The prompts on this book can be copied and pasted, you just need to adjust the words in brackets.

MARKETING PLAN PROMPT

As a professional actively seeking advanced solutions for optimizing my business operations, I find myself drawn towards [SPECIFY PRODUCT/SERVICE]. To fully understand the extensive capabilities, specific functionalities, and overall benefits of your product/service, could you facilitate a comprehensive, personalized demonstration tailored to my business needs? I'm particularly interested in exploring how your product/service can integrate with our existing systems, drive process efficiencies, and contribute to our strategic goals. Additionally, could you also provide insight into your post-purchase support services, including but not limited to customer service, technical assistance, and product upgrades?

CONTENT MARKETING BASIC PROMPT

"Can you help me develop a content marketing strategy that aligns with my company's brand voice [**YOUR COMPANY'S BRAND VOICE**] and target audience [**YOUR TARGET AUDIENCE**]?"

CONTENT MARKETING EXTRA PROMPTS

1. Act as a content marketing specialist for a cooking website. Create a comprehensive blog post outline focused on providing tips and tricks for meal prepping, targeting busy professionals with a conversational tone and a desired length of 1200-1500 words.
2. Act as a content marketing specialist for a fashion brand. Create a comprehensive blog post outline focused on providing

tips and tricks for building a sustainable wardrobe, targeting environmentally conscious consumers with a conversational tone and a desired length of 1200-1500 words.
3. As an experienced copywriter, generate a comprehensive, SEO-optimized blog post outline for the keyword "budget travel hacks", targeting a budget travel audience with a conversational tone and a desired length of 1500-2000 words.
4. As an experienced copywriter, generate a comprehensive, SEO-optimized blog post outline for the keyword "digital marketing trends", targeting a small business audience with a conversational tone and a desired length of 1500-2000 words.
5. As a content strategist, create an editorial calendar for a wellness blog that caters to a millennial audience. The calendar should cover the next six months and include a mix of evergreen and topical content.
6. As a UX writer, write a user interface copy for a mobile banking app that's designed to simplify the banking experience for senior citizens.

7. As a social media manager, develop a social media strategy for a B2B SaaS company looking to increase brand awareness and generate leads through LinkedIn.
8. As a technical writer, create a user manual for a new software product that's designed for non-technical users. The manual should be concise, easy to understand, and cover all the essential features of the product.
9. As a marketing copywriter, write a landing page copy for an e-commerce site selling eco-friendly home products. The copy should be persuasive, SEO-friendly, and focused on the benefits of the products.
10. As a content marketer, develop a content marketing plan for a startup that offers a subscription-based service for remote workers. The plan should cover the next 12 months and include a mix of blog posts, videos, and social media content.
11. As a technical writer experienced in API documentation, write a developer guide for a new API product that's designed for mobile app developers. The guide should be comprehensive, easy to follow, and include code samples.

12. As a copywriter, write an email sequence for a B2C company that sells organic skincare products. The sequence should be persuasive, engaging, and designed to convert subscribers into customers.

13. As a content strategist, develop a content marketing plan for a software company that specializes in cybersecurity. The plan should include a mix of gated and ungated content, and focus on educating potential customers on the importance of cybersecurity.

14. As a freelance writer, write an in-depth article on the benefits of meditation for a health and wellness blog. The article should be well-researched, include expert quotes, and be written in an engaging and informative tone.

15. As an experienced copywriter, generate a comprehensive, SEO-optimized blog post outline for the keyword [X], targeting an [X] audience with a conversational tone and a desired length of 1500-2000 words.

16. Suppose you're a content marketer; create an SEO-optimized blog post outline that compares and contrasts different products or services related to keyword [X], targeting consumers with a

neutral tone and a desired length of 1000-1500 words.
17. As a freelance writer, generate a comprehensive blog post outline that showcases the unique features and benefits of [X], targeting [product] enthusiasts with a persuasive tone and a desired length of 1500-2000 words.
18. As a technical writer experienced in SEO, please create a detailed blog post outline that provides a step-by-step guide for using [X], targeting beginners with a friendly and helpful tone and a desired length of 800-1000 words.
19. Act as a content marketing specialist, create a comprehensive blog post outline focused on providing tips and tricks for [X], targeting DIY enthusiasts with a conversational tone and a desired length of 1200-1500 words.
20. List the main ideas for a blog post about [subject] and present them in a table.
21. To be used in a blog post, outline the critical elements of a detailed guide on [subject]
22. As if you're an experienced content writer. Write seven subheadings for the blog article with the title [title]; the titles should be catchy and 60 characters max.

23. Suppose you're a content marketing specialist, write a thorough outline using a two level heading structure for a blog article titled [title].
24. Act as a social media content writer, analyze this outline [outline], and remove/add parts if necessary to make the blog post more engaging and informative.

BUYING PERSON TO DIGITAL PRODUCT

This Chat GPT prompt it's a framework to create digital product name targeted on specific audience.

Step #1: Identify buying personas

I am thinking about creating [describe your digital product] - can you please map out 5 distinct buying personas?

Step #2: Deep dive into pain points and desires

I want to go with [your selected buying persona]. Can you please dive really deep into their psyche and surface the internal conversation about pain points that my product can help address? What do they actually say to themselves? Give me the internal conversation in bullet points, and show me the full spectrum.

What are their desires and hopes? What would the best solution for this exactly do for them? Please give me a list of all their desires related to the solution. All the little things they wish for.

Step #3: Name your new opportunity

What titles can I give my [container] based on the pain points and desires that present it as the ultimate, new solution? Please give me a long list and keep in mind to keep these short and easy to understand. The immediate benefit should be extremely clear.

Check for:

- Easy to understand
- Raw & real
- The benefit is immediately clear

www.ingramcontent.com/pod-product-compliance
Lightning Source LLC
Chambersburg PA
CBHW070411230526
45471CB00006B/2756